For my precious Munchkins: Ezra, Caxton, and Amos.
Spending time with you boys brings me vitality and endless joy.

Copyright © Moji Taiwo

All rights reserved. No part of this book may be reproduced by any mechanical, photographic, or electronic process or in the form of phonographic recording; nor may it be stored in a retrieval system, transmitted, or otherwise copied for public or private use without the prior written permission of the author at mojitaiwo1@gmail.com.
ISBN (paperback): 978-1-7751235-4-5 / ISBN (Ebook): 978-1-7751235-8-3 / ISBN (IngramSpark): 978-1-7751235-3-8

Moji Taiwo
www.mojitaiwo.com

Grandma took us to the park.
We walked with Grandma to play at the playground.

Grandma said walking is a good exercise for us, because it makes us strong.

We must also hold hands with Grandma to keep her from getting lost.

But wait a minute!
Grandma has only two hands,
and there are three of us with six hands.

"Hmm...How are we going to do this?" Junior Munchkin asked.

"I have an idea," said Senior Munchkin. "I can hold Grandma's left hand, and you can hold her right hand."

"What about Baby Munckin? Who is going to hold his hand?" said Junior Munchkin.

Can you think of other ways to get to the playground?

When we got to the playground, we saw other kids; boys and girls. Some are bigger than us and some are smaller.

We asked the other kids to play with us, and we made new friends.

Grandma said it is good to be nice to other people.

We had fun swinging on the swings with our new friends and sliding on slides, and hanging off monkey bars.

We ran through the castle to the top and looked out the balcony with them.

Grandma also met new friends at the playground.

How do YOU make new friends?

www.ingramcontent.com/pod-product-compliance
Lightning Source LLC
Chambersburg PA
CBHW040023130526
44590CB00036B/73